THE 1950s HOME

Sophie Leighton

English Rose
RECD. TRADE MARK
KITCHEN EQUIPMENT

SHIRE PUBLICATIONS

First published in Great Britain in 2009 by
Shire Publications Ltd, Midland House, West Way, Botley,
Oxford OX2 0PH, United Kingdom.
443 Park Avenue South, New York, NY 10016, USA.
E-mail: shire@shirebooks.co.uk   www.shirebooks.co.uk

A CIP catalogue record for this book is available from the
British Library.

Shire Library no. 488   •   ISBN-13: 978 0 74780 711 7

Sophie Leighton has asserted her right under the
Copyright, Designs and Patents Act, 1988, to be identified
as the author of this book.

Designed by Ken Vail Graphic Design, Cambridge, UK and
typeset in Perpetua and Gill Sans.
Printed in China Through Worldprint Ltd.

09 10 11 12 13   10 9 8 7 6 5 4 3 2 1

COVER IMAGE
Fitting pelmets to a 1950s living room. Note the
contemporary heating, large windows, and sparse decor.

TITLE PAGE IMAGE
An advertisement from 1952 for an English Rose fitted
kitchen.

CONTENTS PAGE IMAGE
A 1952 advertisement for a Royal Venton fireplace,
designed to be 'in perfect harmony with your home.'

ACKNOWLEDGEMENTS
I would like to thank my family for supporting this project,
as well as colleagues at the Victoria and Albert Museum,
and all those who wrote and told me about their
experiences of the 1950s.

I would also like to thank those who allowed me to use
their illustrations, which are acknowledged as follows:

Avoncroft Museum, pages 16, and 17 (bottom);
Black and Decker, page 44 (bottom);
Nora Blagburn, page 41 (bottom); Mike Byrne
(http://aghs.virtualbrum.co.uk/agww2/prefabs), page
17 (top); Caroline Cleevely, page 52 (bottom); CVW
Limited, page 45 (bottom); The Daily Mail, pages 3, 11
(bottom), 25 (top), 30, 34, 48 (top), 50 (top), and 53;
Mr and Mrs J. B. Dastur, page 21; Denby, page 49;
Ron Eatwell, page 15 (top and bottom); Formica Group,
page 47 (top); G-plan (www.gplan.co.uk, and
www.gplancabinets.co.uk), page 40 (top); Wyn Grant,
page 52 (top right); Rachel Grantham, page 51;
Charles Hewitt/Picture Post/Getty Images, page 6 (top);
Hoover Candy Group, page 29 (bottom); Mrs Hulls, pages
18 (top), and 52 (top left); Imerys Minerals Ltd, page 18
(bottom); Lewisham Local History Centre, page 11 (top);
Albert McCabe/Hulton Archive/Getty Images, page
8; Tim McMahon, page 10 (bottom); Edward
Miller/Keystone/Getty Images, page 14; Museum of
Domestic Design & Architecture, Middlesex University,
pages 6 (bottom), 7 (bottom), 10 (top), 13 (top and
bottom), 26, 42, 44, 45 (top), 46 (top), and 47 (bottom);
Museum of Kent Life, pages 29 (top), 32 (top), and 48
(bottom); National Grid plc., pages 26 (top), and 27
(top); Rural Life Centre, Tilford, page 36 (top right);
Peter Stackpole/Time & Life Pictures/Getty Images, page
20; Stevenage Museum, pages 12, 25 (bottom), and 32
(bottom); Tradestyle Cabinets Ltd. English Rose Kitchens
are still produced at the time of printing, title page, page
24 (bottom); University of Brighton Design Archives, page
7 (top); and Michael Viner, page 11 (top).

Shire Publications is supporting the Woodland Trust, the UK's leading woodland conservation charity, by funding the dedication of trees.

CONTENTS

INTRODUCTION

H OMES transformed dramatically in the 1950s: post-war Britain was ready for change, and housing was at the forefront of the mind of the regenerating nation. There were vast house-building programmes, council estates, New Towns, prefabs, and advanced technology that promised to save time and energy. Fridges, central heating and electric lighting all became common; modern living as we know it began then, and the government encouraged people to think about their houses and what went into them.

But it was not an easy decade: as well as the lingering effects of the two recent world wars, the 1950s witnessed the war against communist North Korea (1950–3), the Suez Canal crisis (1956), the Cold War and the disintegration of the British Empire. Rationing was still in place, and racism was rife. At the start of the 1950s, as foreign currency became more expensive, the cost of imports rose. There were shortages of building materials and a reduced workforce to construct new homes.

As many as a third of British homes had been seriously damaged or demolished in the war, resulting in a desperate need for new accommodation. This shortage, exacerbated by the increase in marriages and births, ensured housing in Britain was a priority throughout the 1950s.

The Labour government, elected in 1945, prioritised public support of home building. It established the welfare state in 1945, creating the National Health Service in 1948, and nationalised the coal, steel, gas, electricity and railway industries. Homes remained on the political agenda when the Conservatives gained power in 1951, although the emphasis shifted to support private housing.

Homes and home design became important to the nation. The government knew that it needed to keep morale high as the economy and society at large recovered. Ignoring criticism over such an extravagant event, in 1951 it staged the Festival of Britain, a century after the Great Exhibition lauded international industrial design in London's Hyde Park.

At once a cultural funfair and a serious exposition of what art and design could achieve, the Festival of Britain was a celebration of culture and British

Opposite:
The 1950s home became associated with both national and individual identity, as bold new colours and textures replaced the more restrained styles of the previous decade.

5

history, industry, hopes and identity. It was a way of promoting good design values, suggesting ways in which Britain and British architecture could move forward. It highlighted town planning – a key concern at that time due to the housing shortage. The festival director, Gerald Barry, pronounced it a 'tonic to the nation'. It stimulated British manufacturing industries and pointed people away from the past and towards the technology-based future.

Left: Photograph of Coventry taken on 5 November 1956 showing the reconstruction of the city centre following the air raid of November 1940, which destroyed the cathedral and surrounding area.

Below: South Bank Exhibition plan from the Festival of Britain, 1951.

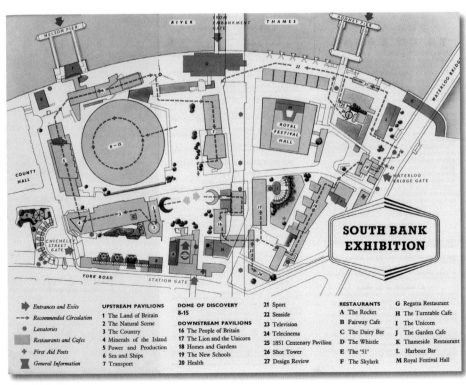

SOUTH BANK EXHIBITION

	UPSTREAM PAVILIONS	DOME OF DISCOVERY	21 Sport	RESTAURANTS	G Regatta Restaurant
▶ Entrances and Exits	1 The Land of Britain	8-15	22 Seaside	A The Rocket	H The Turntable Cafe
- -▶ Recommended Circulation	2 The Natural Scene	DOWNSTREAM PAVILIONS	23 Television	B Fairway Cafe	I The Unicorn
● Lavatories	3 The Country	16 The People of Britain	24 Telecinema	C The Dairy Bar	J The Garden Cafe
Restaurants and Cafes	4 Minerals of the Island	17 The Lion and the Unicorn	25 1851 Centenary Pavilion	D The Whistle	K Thameside Restaurant
✚ First Aid Posts	5 Power and Production	18 Homes and Gardens	26 Shot Tower	E The '51'	L Harbour Bar
▮ General Information	6 Sea and Ships	19 The New Schools	27 Design Review	F The Skylark	M Royal Festival Hall
	7 Transport	20 Health			

Towns throughout Britain were encouraged to organise events and exhibitions to celebrate the festival. The main site was on the South Bank of London's River Thames where the new cultural centre, the Royal Festival Hall, was sited. Everyone knew about it, and it did have a profound influence. Between May and September 1951, 8.5 million people visited the Festival.

An impression by Roger Nicholson of part of the Home Centre Interior

The Festival gave a fantastical glimpse of modern design. It gave hope to those living in poor housing conditions, and offered tips on how to make homes brighter and easier to live in. It showcased new technology and the work of key designers such as Robin and Lucienne Day. The Days were each celebrated in their own right; Robin for his modern furniture made of materials such as steel and plywood, and Lucienne for her striking textile designs. Whilst the festival extolled Britain to the point of being unashamedly propagandistic, it also succeeded in encouraging people to think about their homes and the way they lived. For those lucky enough to have a home of their own at that time, it gave them the impetus to make theirs one to be proud of.

Interior of the new Design Centre, 1956.

Good design was considered a panacea and was widely fostered. Alongside initiatives such as the Festival, the Board of Trade had established the Council of Industrial Design (COID) in 1944 to promote British trade at home and abroad, to counter American competition and rebuild the export market. It had organised the Britain Can Make It exhibition at the Victoria and Albert Museum in 1946 to publicise the best in British design, and from 1949 produced the magazine *Design* to encourage good design. The Design Centre opened in London in 1956, as a venue to display the COID's 'index' of examples of successful design.

'Stella', wallpaper designed by Lucienne Day for Cole & Sons, 1951.

America had an increasingly powerful influence over Britain. New and fast-changing design was used in the States to stimulate consumerism, rather than to guide ethical values. As Britain emerged from the hardships of rationing in the earlier part of the decade, it came under the sway of Americanisation and consumer culture. British people were progressively able to indulge in this as incomes rose. During the decade the average weekly wage almost doubled, from £6 8s. 0d. to £11 2s. 6d., while income tax fell. British consumers looked to high street stores, from the trendsetting Heals to the everyday Woolworths, to bring them the range of décor and designs they wanted for their homes.

TOWN PLANNING AND ARCHITECTURAL STYLES

HOW DID BRITAIN cope with the 1950s housing shortage? Homes became more economical. There was a range of architectural styles, but the newly built homes were designed to be compact and straightforward. Much of the thinking behind the planning had been done before the war, using the principles of modernist architecture of the 1920s and '30s. In the 1950s, making best use of space and keeping to simple designs and materials made sense for all homes, regardless of whether they were built by individuals or the state.

In post-war Britain, 1.46 million homes were needed, particularly in urban areas. In London alone, 100,000 families had lost their homes due to bombings. In the north of England, new housing was needed where new industries developed – when new coal mines opened, new towns had to be built nearby. New homes were also needed throughout Britain to improve the overall standard of housing and the health of the nation. Slums were cleared, and were replaced by new and safer housing. Between 1955 and 1965, 600,000 dwellings were demolished.

Compared with earlier decades, in the early 1950s materials were short and labour was scarce. The rental market that had dominated in the early twentieth century, with 90 per cent of homes rented in the 1920s, declined in the 1940s and '50s.

By 1950 about 60 per cent of houses were owner-occupied. Landlords sold off their stock and were reluctant to invest in new property, despite government incentives. The government subsidised local authority housing: from 1945 to 1951, 89 per cent of the 1.01 million houses that were built in Great Britain were local authority dwellings. From 1951, however, the Conservative government encouraged private housing. Between 1951 and 1956 over 1.9 million houses were built, bringing the total to over 2.5 million new houses.

TOWN PLANNING

Town planning dominated Britain's restructure. Building new housing and regenerating existing dwellings was an opportunity to improve living and

Opposite:
A high-rise block of flats under construction in Glasgow. The tenements that had formerly occupied the site were among the worst slums in Britain and there had been campaigns to redevelop the area for many years before work finally began in the late fifties.

A new build
in Brimsdown,
Enfield, 1958,
showing a house
exterior typical
of the time, with
a mixture of brick,
glass, concrete and
tiled surfaces.

working conditions. In Britain, architects and planners were strongly influenced by utopian ideals rooted in the nineteenth century: people believed that better-planned housing could lead to better societies. The Briton Ebenezer Howard (1850–1928), who published *Gardens of Tomorrow* in 1902 and developed Welwyn and Letchworth Garden Cities, advocated the placement of towns away from the city core, in self-contained communities of mixed classes. Spurred on by social concerns to eliminate Victorian slums, Howard idealised the creation of new towns outside of the city centre.

A row of terraced
'back to back'
pit houses
in Chopwell,
Newcastle, c. 1958.

In Paris, Le Corbusier developed equally influential ideas. Having concentrated largely on private modernist projects and theoretical city plans before the war, in the 1940s he focused on urban housing, endorsing high-rise living as an economic way of using city space.

The 1947 Town and Country Planning Act promoted a centralised system of planning in Britain. Local authorities were given more control over what was built in their area, both privately and publicly. The government-led strategy aimed to tackle war-stricken towns that needed rebuilding, as well as creating the so-called 'New Towns' – completely new housing developments in green but urban settings. Professional planner Patrick Abercrombie realised his dream after the war in his 1945

Lammas Green Estate, Lewisham, when it first opened in 1957, with inhabitant Muriel Coates being greeted by the Mayor.

Greater London Plan. He planned to move over a million habitants from inner London to the new satellite towns. Parallel to this, more green land was protected than ever before, such as the Green Belt around London, designated National Parks, and other ring-fenced areas.

The New Towns Act (1946) resulted in the establishment of eleven new towns between 1946 and 1955, eight of which were developed to house Londoners on the outskirts of the city. Other towns were built in order to tackle poor housing in areas of existing employment. The first of the new towns was Stevenage (designated in 1946), followed by Crawley, Aycliffe, Harlow and Hemel Hempstead (1947), Peterlee, Welwyn Garden City and Hatfield (1948), Basildon and Bracknell (1949), and Corby (1950).

In the 1950s, as major cities in developing countries were swelling with people moving in from the countryside (for example Cairo, Mexico City and Shanghai), in the developed world, cities such as London and New York were shrinking as inhabitants moved out to the suburbs and satellite towns. The British government advocated new towns as modern, affordable and convenient places to live. It encouraged people to move to them with the promise of new homes and jobs, making provisions for new residents to start their lives afresh.

But moving to the new towns was a mixed blessing. People fondly remember the swish new buildings fitted out with contemporary conveniences and good insulation, heating, lighting and plumbing.

A house exhibited at the 1958 Daily Mail Ideal Home Show. The show influenced British home design and content throughout the 1950s.

11

A kitchen in a new house at Leaves Spring in Stevenage, 1953, with gas cooker and butler sink aligned to create an efficient working space, and a wide modern window positioned to give maximum light.

At a time when getting a new home was a desperate and lengthy business, involving waiting lists and lots of luck even for the middle classes, these new houses must have been a dream. Many new inhabitants, however, felt isolated from their home ground, their family and friends.

As well as focusing on housing in new suburbs, local councils began to restructure inner city housing. In London for example, London County Council (LCC) stormed ahead with a building programme, obtaining large areas of land and constructing vast council estates using the latest designs and technology. Many of these were finished in the 1950s.

EARLY 1950s: LOCAL AUTHORITY NEW BUILDS

Good design was a paramount concern for council buildings, but since finding the right materials was a challenge, designs were economical. After the war and up until the early 1950s, steel was unavailable in convenient forms. The LCC, for example, was proud of its ability to improvise, using steel channels salvaged from Anderson shelters, which were welded together to form joist sections.

Housing estates were envisaged (as described in an LCC brochure) to offer a reasonable variety of accommodation. Each estate was made up of small high-rise apartments for smaller families, and larger, lower units with gardens, intended as family homes. Each building was made to the type plan of the council. The brochure boasted 'good space standards' for post-war housing. This was important at a time when rooms were getting smaller and even the standard height of rooms was lowered due to building costs, supply of materials and attempts to limit heating bills.

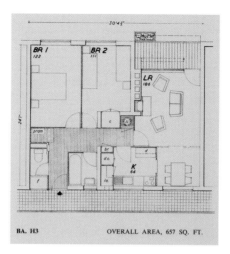

BA. H3   OVERALL AREA, 657 SQ. FT.

LCC housing type plan for two-bedroom flat BA.H3, 1956. The living room and kitchen are linked by a dining area.

LCC housing type plan for three-bedroom terraced home TH.Q4N, 1956.

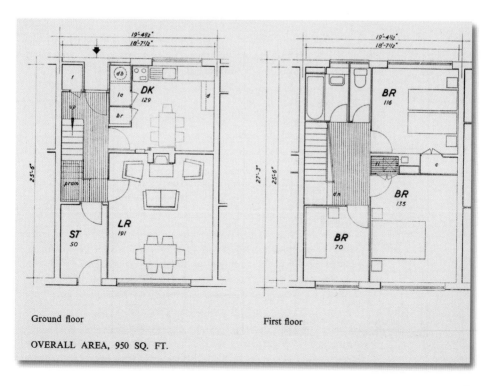

Ground floor

First floor

OVERALL AREA, 950 SQ. FT.

13

Council houses were good value for the time but still rather expensive. On the Alton Estate, in Roehampton in London in 1959, new council homes cost on average £2,240 to build, and were let at subsidised prices.

Alex Morley-Smith, writing in the *Daily Mail Ideal Home Book* of 1951–2, waxes lyrical about his new council home. Initially when a friend suggested moving to a council home, he had experienced a 'chilling vision of vast grey six-storied council flats in the gloomier suburbs…' This concept, however, vanished quickly. He describes his new house as having:

> a simple friendly face, entirely in character with its purpose. The brick-work is of soft variegated reds, the roof tiles of darker red. The floor plans…show how its essential 'domestic' character is carried indoors. Downstairs, the maximum use is made of the extra space which 'whole house heating' [a furnace in the kitchen] allows: there is no hall passage, just a small draught-hall opening into the living-room out of which the dining-room/play-room opens behind folding doors. Upstairs, of the four bedrooms, the three smaller ones will allow many alternative uses as the family grows up.

The new council high-rise flats were greeted less effusively. Tower blocks were a means of providing standardised housing, condensed and cost-effective, and constructed with modern materials such as steel and concrete.

They were made up of multiple identical units. Park Hill in Sheffield, for example, built from 1959–66, included a nineteen-storey block containing 678 flats. Research carried out by the Geffrye Museum draws attention to tenants' dissatisfaction. A radio programme, *The Flats,* broadcast on 2 July 1959, looked at an unidentified LCC North London estate. The land had previously housed 1,500 in poor overcrowded conditions and now housed 1,700 to agreed minimum standards. Tenants disliked the 'cold new feeling' of the high-rise, and the sensation of being 'boxed in'. Rents were quite high, and many women had to go out to work, leaving the high-rise deserted in the daytime. Despite these problems, many tenants appreciated the improved living conditions – heating, a bath, indoor toilet, washing facilities and a balcony.

PRIVATE HOUSING

By the late 1950s, more homes were privately owned. Most new homes built by commercial contractors such as Wates followed the council's lead with simple, efficient and flexible house design. £2,000 was the average cost of a three-bedroom house, and a young couple needed an income of £15 per week to afford it. A St Albans resident spent £1,800 on her first family home (a Victorian terraced house) in 1959. It took twenty years to pay the mortgage off. At that time, fixed-rate mortgages requiring as little as 10 per cent deposit were available. The council offered

This is one of the cheques to Davis contractors for the purchase of a house. Mr and Mrs Eatwell signed up to a new house at the annual Daily Mail Ideal Home Show, and paid in instalments over two years before they moved in, in 1955.

The Eatwells' house built by Davis Contractors in 1955 in Claygate, Surrey.

improvement grants for houses in need of updating, to enable new owners to install a bathroom and inside toilet.

Despite the growing number of new buildings, most private housing consisted of existing older styles, mainly Georgian, Victorian, Edwardian, and 1930s-type houses, conversions or refurbishments. Much of the shell of these houses remained unchanged, although the interiors were modernised by means of new heating systems and décor.

CONVERSIONS

Due to the housing shortage, many of the large, privately owned Georgian and Victorian houses were converted into bedsits, particularly in London. Renting a room was often the only option for many who had no capital to buy a home and were ineligible, or on the very long waiting list, for council housing. The government struggled to improve conditions for those renting rooms, offering improvement grants of up to 50 per cent to landlords renovating or converting a property, on condition that the local authority then fixed the rent. Many houses had little plumbing. Landlords could be extremely prescriptive, even specifying the day of the week when tenants could take a bath. Professional singles could afford the best rooms, whilst poorer citizens, including black people from former British colonies, restricted by rampant racism, had very little choice and had to suffer cramped, expensive housing.

PREFABS

While permanent new homes were being built and existing housing brought up to modern standards, prefabricated homes were intended as a quick solution to the housing problem – and far removed from the sordid bedsit. They were temporary homes with a fixed shelf life, but many remained in use

The Arcon Mk.V Prefab at Avoncroft Museum, originally built in 1946. The Arcon Mk.V was made with a steel frame clad with asbestos cement sheeting.

A Phoenix prefab (asbestos-clad like the Arcon Mk.V style), in Wake Green Road, Birmingham, built in the late 1940s. This style was promoted by the contractors Laing, McAlpine and Henry Boot and echoed a traditional house, with central front door, chimney piece, and pitched roof. These buildings were given a Grade II listing in 1998.

for over fifty years. As early as 1944 Winston Churchill had begun the 'Temporary Housing Programme'. Factories that once made aircraft and armaments were used to make prefabs, with 500,000 houses planned, of which 156,623 were actually constructed. There was a series of designs, based on a prototype by the Ministry of Works. Most were detached bungalows, the aluminium version being the most popular.

Prefab homes were relatively economical, quick to produce and easy to build. Every compact house had an entrance hall, two bedrooms with built-in wardrobes, a heated bathroom, fitted kitchen, a living room and a small garden. Since they had to be transported by road, no component could be wider than 7.5 feet. The total floor space in a prefab was 635 square feet. They were fitted

A kitchen dated to 1947, as displayed in Avoncroft Museum's prefab, revealing a bright and clean interior packed with modern conveniences.

17

with mains electricity, hot and cold running water, a toilet, and a built-in refrigerator. The kitchen and bathroom were positioned back to back to ensure ease of plumbing.

People who moved into prefabs, the majority of whom were working class, were dismayed at the buildings' odd appearance and cramped spaces, and complained about the thin walls and resulting cold and condensation. This was countered by the modern facilities and private plots of garden, which were an unexpected luxury and led to prefabs being known as 'Palaces for the People'.

Above: Prefabs in Greenhundred Road, Peckham, in the early 1950s, with well-kept garden plots.

BUILT·TO PLEASE AND TO LAST

Cornish Unit

HOUSES

O RIGINALLY designed to meet the housing needs of mid-Cornwall, the Cornish Unit house has demonstrated its suitability for any locality. The concrete units are made in factories from Cornish Quartz and can quickly be erected on available building sites with a minimum of skilled labour. Details of these and other plan types of dwellings available will gladly be sent on application to the address below—

Cornish Unit houses used construction methods developed for prefabricated housing.

SELLECK, NICHOLLS & COMPANY, LTD.,
EAST HILL, ST. AUSTELL, CORNWALL.
Telephone: ST. AUSTELL 1071.
(A Subsidiary of English Clays, Lovering, Pochin & Co., Ltd.)

Prefabrication was used in private housing too. Due to the shortage of traditional materials such as bricks in the 1940s and early '50s, pre-cast concrete panels were used in house construction. 'Cornish Unit Construction Houses' and 'Airey Houses' are examples of affordable, mass-produced private housing that used prefabricated elements.

LATER IN THE DECADE: PRIVATE NEW-BUILDS

Following the austerity of the earlier part of the decade when house building was severely restricted, as the economy recovered the market for new architect-designed houses grew. *House and Garden* magazine (January 1955) proclaims:

Practical Householder boasts that this bungalow is 'An Architect-designed £2,000 Dwelling Which May be Built for Under £1,000 by any Handyman.'

> At last we are free to build again – licences have been abolished, restrictions relaxed, and material shortages are almost non-existent. Once again we can dream of, plan, and create, our perfect home, a house exactly suited to our own and our family's needs....

House and Garden outlines the components that make a modern British home, which echo the main elements of the new council designs:

> The houses we plan today, and will build tomorrow, can have more light, more living and storage space, better services, greater built-in comfort and convenience for living....We can now build in new ways, using new materials; steel, concrete, and glass, added to brick and timber, enlarge the traditional range and encourage new forms better suited to our changed ways of life.

British architects were influenced by American and Scandinavian houses. One high-profile project was the 'Case Study Houses' in the USA, which ran from 1944 to 1966. *Arts & Architecture* magazine sponsored some of the best American architects of the day such as Richard Neutra, Raphael Soriano, Craig Ellwood, Charles and Ray Eames and Pierre Koenig, to design and build affordable and efficient model homes, intended to be copied on a large scale. These buildings were mainly built with brick, steel, aluminium, glass and concrete, were one-storey high and characterised by a great deal of light with flexible living spaces. Many incorporated industrially produced components, confirming prefabrication as a modern way of lowering housing costs.

Exterior view of the Eames's house in Pacific Palisades, California (August 1950), part of the Case Study House Program sponsored by *Art & Architecture* magazine. The house consists of two cubes, and was designed initially by Charles Eames and Eero Saarinen and later amended by Charles Eames and his wife Ray Eames.

Ideal Home and Gardening (January 1955) promotes a new house 'with four star features: no doors downstairs, smooth-flowing floor plan, central-source heating and built-in decoration.' At the end of the decade *Ideal Home* (July 1959) features the architectural practice of Austin Smith. His modern house extols:

> greater use of glass ... more light ... maximum exploitation of land (hence terrace building) ... spaciousness despite limited size ... decisive use of built-ins [fitted furniture] ... increased privacy [by use of flexible screening] in spite of maximum use of glass ... [and] a high standard of heating and insulation.

New builds in the modern style were of course an extravagance, and although they could be built for as little as £2,000 in the 1950s, a family home could easily cost over £4,000. They were perceived to be for the trendier middle classes, and far less cosy than the traditional British home.

EXTERIOR FIXTURES AND FITTINGS

Façades of 1950s houses were typified by their combination of panels of brick, wood and glass. Weatherboarding, tile hanging or rendering was frequently used on brickwork, and had the advantage of increasing insulation.

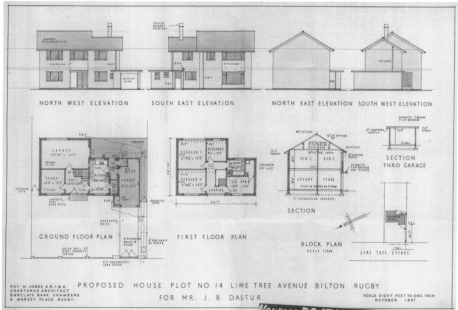

NORTH WEST ELEVATION   SOUTH EAST ELEVATION   NORTH EAST ELEVATION   SOUTH WEST ELEVATION

SECTION THRO GARAGE

SECTION

GROUND FLOOR PLAN   FIRST FLOOR PLAN   BLOCK PLAN

PROPOSED HOUSE. PLOT NO. 14. LIME TREE AVENUE. BILTON. RUGBY.

FOR MR. J. B. DASTUR.

ROY M. JONES A.R.I.B.A. CHARTERED ARCHITECT BARCLAYS BANK CHAMBERS 6 MARKET PLACE. RUGBY.

SCALE EIGHT FEET TO ONE INCH OCTOBER 1957

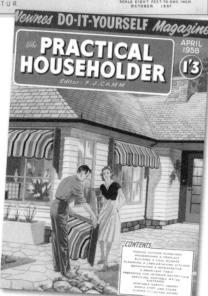

Above: These plans for a privately commissioned four-bedroom house in Rugby (1957) show fashionable features such as exterior rendering and flat windows. The ground floor is quite compact, and it does have mod cons such as central heating (oil). Although this was designed quite late in the decade, the kitchen is fitted with a larder rather than a fridge.

Right: This house shows typical 1950s features such as weatherboarding.

Roofs were shallow pitched or flat. Guttering was still made with ironwork manufactured in the great industrial centres such as Birmingham. Plastic guttering would be for the future.

Although many houses retained older wooden windows, new windows were increasingly made of metal. Metal windows became subject to British Standard Specification by 1945, so that there were fewer sizes and designs, and installation became cheaper. Compared to previous styles, 1950s windows were much wider, with a series of vertical panes. Michael Farr in *Design in British Industry: A mid-century survey* (1955) is pleased with the vertical emphasis as it is 'better suited to man, who habitually stands upright.'

MODERN SPACES

HOMES BECAME SMALLER in the 1950s and contained fewer rooms. As a result, each room necessarily became a much more flexible space. Previously, houses were generally large, with high ceilings and spacious hallways and entrance halls. Victorian and Edwardian houses, for example (dependent on cost of course), typically consisted of a kitchen, a scullery for food preparation and washing clothes, one or two parlours for receiving guests and carrying out tasks (such as sewing), a dining room, a study, a bathroom and bedrooms. Each room had a distinct function.

By the end of the 1950s, the average family home consisted of three bedrooms, a bathroom with toilet, a living room, and a kitchen or kitchen-diner. Often family houses had a garden, sometimes with a conservatory to provide extra space. Areas were cleverly combined. Sometimes beds were hidden behind folding screens, enabling a dual-use living room and bedroom to resemble a standard living room during the day.

In the contemporary compact house, the kitchen and scullery were combined. The parlour, traditionally used as a spare 'best' room, began to vanish from house plans, or was fused with the dining room. Architects doubted that people actually used the parlour often enough to justify its presence. They encouraged the living room as a multi-purpose space, doubling up to receive guests, eat and play in.

Multi-purpose rooms were not ideal, however. Aside from having less space, many regretted the loss of separate rooms for specific uses. Open-plan kitchen-diners meant that cooking smells could pervade the whole house – cookers were therefore fitted with extractor fans.

TECHNOLOGY
In the 1950s technological developments in the home became cheaper and more widely available to ordinary householders. They influenced how houses were organised and lived in. Plumbing became commonplace, which enabled an increased number of homes to have in-built bathrooms and toilets – formerly this was a luxury reserved for those who could afford it.

Opposite:
A kitchen featuring the latest in modern technology. The clean lines and lino flooring in both parts of the room contribute to a sense of space and cleanliness.

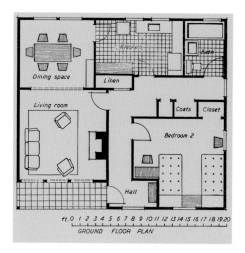

GROUND FLOOR PLAN

After 1945, most houses relied almost exclusively on electricity rather than gas to heat, light and power their homes. Even though electricity was more expensive, it was considered cleaner and more efficient, and by 1951 almost 90 per cent of all households were connected to the National Grid.

Home heating advanced greatly in the 1950s. Previously it was provided by fires in one or two of the rooms at ground level, with no heating upstairs. Rooms were commonly frosty and homeowners lamented the harsh winters. In the 1950s, different methods of heating became common as incomes increased and heating became affordable.

Above: In this plan of the ground floor of a typical family house, you can see the efficient use of space, such as the combined dining-living room, and the bathroom and kitchen positioned back to back, to make plumbing easier.

Right: Ingenious ways of incorporating living, cooking and dining in a single room were promoted widely in magazines.

Above: This living room wall slides back to reveal the bedroom. Folding doors like these were exhibited at the 1955 Daily Mail Ideal Home Show.

Left: Space is cleverly maximised in this stylish home at Half Hyde, Shephall, Stevenage (c. 1957), where the living room is divided from the dining area by a low partition.

25

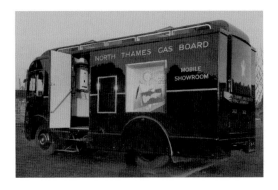

Due to the competition from electricity, gas appliances were widely promoted in the 1950s.

Extensive heating remained rare in older houses. Victorian and 1930s buildings still used solid fuel fires in the living or dining room and a fire or grate in the kitchen. Often one fire might be connected to a back boiler to heat water and sometimes one or two radiators. The Clean Air Act of 1957 banned coal fires in smokeless zones. This meant that more people chose to replace open fires with more efficient slow-burning coke or anthracite stoves, which as well as being cleaner, had doors to retain the heat for longer.

In rooms that were less used, homeowners turned to small heaters powered by gas, paraffin or electricity. Heating was increasingly electric, despite the expense. Living rooms were often installed with electric heaters, with back-up portable heaters fuelled by paraffin.

It became more common for water to be heated electrically, although solid fuel boilers were still very common in the 1950s. Electric immersion heaters gradually replaced coal-fired systems, but these were often supplemented by an economical instantaneous gas or electric water-heater for kitchen or bathroom use, which heated water up as and when it was needed.

Central heating was all the rage in the new builds, although still rare in the 1950s home. Only 5 per cent of households had central heating by 1960. New council housing had central or 'partial' heating installed as a matter of course. The living room was fitted with a radiator (with water heated by electricity), with pipes providing heat to other rooms.

In the 1950s there were novel ways of heating the house. The warm air method was advocated as being modern and convenient. Air was heated by solid fuel, gas or oil, controlled by a thermostat, and led through pipes into ducts fitted in each room, providing a circulation of warm air throughout the house. Ceiling heating was also trialled, whereby coils of resistance wire were embedded into special plaster in the ceiling, connected to thermostats and fused. The heat radiated into the room below. It was supposed to give the impression of being heated by sunlight, but often

'Switch on to Comfort: A Handbook on Electric Heaters', *Good Housekeeping*, c. 1955.

people found their heads got too hot! The same system of heating the floor was more successful.

Insulation was heavily promoted. Homeowners themselves could install loft insulation, in the form of small vermiculite granules that were simply poured onto the loft cavity.

Lighting in the 1950s evolved in line with the trend for more flexibility in home design. Whereas previously one central light with a big lampshade may have been the only source of illumination in a room, in the 1950s lighting was designed to be practical and adjustable. The expensive move to electricity and the use of wall sockets eased this shift.

In modern homes central room lights often remained, but were set at different levels as appropriate – low lighting to illuminate a living space perhaps, and bright lights in the kitchen. The *News of the World Better Homes Book* (c. 1954) advocated 60 watts for lights in the hall, 125 watts

Above: A range of gas appliances promoted by the Gas Board in 1956, including instantaneous heaters positioned at the back of the van.

Left: Modern lighting was key to contemporary interior design in the 1950s. The range of available designs increased greatly with demand.

in the living room, and 200 watts in the kitchen. Dimmer switches were introduced. Uplighting became more popular, eliminating strong shadows and providing a more sympathetic effect. Small, focused lights, which could be angled, were placed throughout the house at different levels. Adjustable lights for reading or working were more common. In the living room the new fluorescent lights were sometimes used for decoration, to highlight curtains for example. Pull-down lights were popular above dining tables.

The range of cookers on sale increased greatly in the 1950s, just one of the examples of wider consumer choice.

A utility room in the 1950s, showing ironing board and iron, and a drying rack from the 1930s, still very much in use.

Both traditional and modern light designs were widely used, depending on the style of the home. Cast-iron designs such as lanterns, popular before the war, remained in common use. Antique forms – for example, a pendant with plastic candles fitted with small cloth shades – were also popular. Contemporary lampshades were no longer made of frilly fabric. They were increasingly made out of newly available materials in modern designs and shapes. There were lanterns made of cellulose or paper, blown glass bowls in milky or coloured varieties, paper or cloth drums and concertina-hat shades.

As the decade progressed the available range of appliances for the home grew. The consumer magazine *Which?* was first published in 1957 to guide people through their purchases in an ever-expanding market. Women were told by the press that they could 'have it all'. From the 1930s, paid home help rapidly became outdated (domestic workers had become both hard to come by and unaffordable). Women were told they could still combine being the perfect housewife with going out to work – managing to balance housekeeping, childcare and employment. New appliances abounded to help the 1950s housewife with household chores. Vacuum cleaners made a huge difference and 72 per cent of households owned one by 1963. More people could afford to have their own washing machines, and twin tubs were highly desirable.

Here's freedom from all your washday chores . . .

Left:
Washing machines greatly eased housework. This is an advertisement for a Hoovermatic twin tub; an automatic machine with two agitating drums, one for soaping the clothes, and one for rinsing and spinning them dry.

A new kitchen
at the 1950 Daily
Mail Ideal Home
Show, showing
a stylish kitchen
range. Note the
directional lighting
too, focusing
on the cooker.

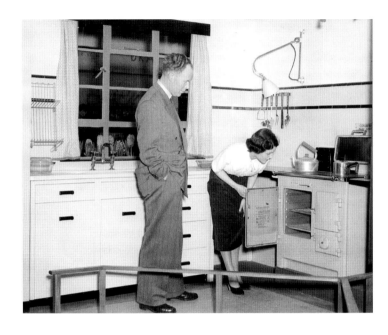

THE KITCHEN

Many of the technological changes in the 1950s materialised in the kitchen. The new ranges such as the Aga, introduced in the 1930s, became fashionable and more easily obtainable, and had the added advantage of heating water as well as cooking food. Kitchen technology such as electric cookers became more prevalent, and so more families were able to invest in them. New materials were prevalent – sinks were made out of modern stainless steel rather than heavy ceramics.

Refrigerators became more widely used. Homeowners invested in them, and councils began to rent them out to tenants. The range and choice expanded – there were even sought-after coloured models. Most ran on electricity. Outside of London, fridges were more unusual and great use was still made of the larder.

Since families ate more frequently (and informally) in the kitchen, its use changed from being a space to prepare food, to one of working, eating and socialising. In the 1950s the press promoted the American dream of a fitted kitchen. Like many home ideals, this had been pushed from as early as the 1930s but it was only in the 1950s, when mass production enabled

One way to
modernise a
kitchen was to
install a stainless
steel sink.

If you are
modernising
your kitchen

There is a Fisholow Stainless
Steel or Vitreous Enamelled
Bowl or Sink to meet all
kitchen requirements.
Simple to install. Easy to
keep clean. Obtainable from
all the leading plumbers and
builders merchants.

FISHOLOW

SHER & LUDLOW LTD. · BIRMINGHAM 2

cheaper units to come onto the market, that the fitted kitchen was adopted on a large scale. Householders were encouraged to think of fitted kitchens as both time- and space-saving.

An example of a fitted kitchen, promoted as an ingenious space- and time-saving solution in 1950s homes.

Women had less time at home and so efficiency was vital: house design could help or hinder. *House and Garden* magazine (February 1956) advised:

> [the planning of a new kitchen] determines whether or not kitchen chores are increased or eased, therefore the correct positioning of the three major centres of the kitchen must be of prime importance. The sink, cooker and refrigerator should form a pattern so that the 'work-flow' becomes a triangle between these points.

THE LIVING ROOM

The use and focus of living rooms was evolving thanks to the new invention of television and changes in heating and lighting. Traditionally, the fireplace was an important feature of the living room. In the 1950s it became even more of a decorative statement, with the addition of ceramic tiles. People ornamented their mantelpiece (and the house in general) sparsely, in contrast to historical tendencies, and the central focus of the room shifted away from the hearth as central heating became more widely used. Echoing Scandinavian homes, windows and curtains (or blinds) often became more prominent.

Right: A living room arranged with all attention on the television.

Below: A living room in Stevenage in 1958, showing the fireplace as a decorative feature, made redundant by the gas heater in front.

Televisions became a feature: in the early 1950s only 3 per cent of households owned a television, but by 1958 it had overtaken radio as the principal form of domestic entertainment, and by 1965 ownership had increased to 85 per cent of households. People were encouraged to adopt a cinematic layout, with a row of chairs or a sofa placed directly in front of the television.

The highlights of this children's room include the cosy rug on a vinyl floor, modern blinds, and a durable space-saving bunk bed.

THE BEDROOM

Bedrooms in the 1950s were characterised by the use of fitted furniture and matching suites of bedside tables. Fitted wardrobes made best use of space, and were practical and affordable. New central heating was rarely installed as far as the bedroom and so people used fabrics to create a feeling of warmth and luxury. Fitted carpets steadily replaced cold linoleum flooring.

THE BATHROOM

Bathrooms became bigger and brighter in the 1950s. Before this they may not even have existed in many houses, the bath being temporarily brought in from an outside yard on bath day (once a week) and filled in the kitchen. Toilets had previously been placed outside, often shared between neighbours, but now at last people of all classes began to be able to have their own baths and indoor toilets. The bath and toilet were not installed in the same room – the toilet was usually placed in a small, separate room adjacent to the bathroom.

Below: Colourful bathroom suites, perhaps with a heated towel rail, took bathroom luxury to new levels.

colour in the bathroom

Shanks

SHANKS & CO. LTD., MANUFACTURERS OF SANITARY APPLIANCES, TUBAL WORKS, BARRHEAD, SCOTLAND
Also at London, Manchester, Newcastle-on-Tyne, Glasgow, Belfast and Dublin

FURNITURE

MOST new householders in the 1950s moved into their homes with the furniture they already owned from the 1940s and before. Any furniture bought new between 1943 and 1952 was likely to be government-sanctioned 'Utility' furniture. Utility furniture was issued via a permit only to those in need, such as newly-weds or those who had suffered bomb damage, and was purchased with coupons or 'units' from a standard catalogue. Sixty units were issued per permit, with a wardrobe 'costing' eight units, and a standard upright chair one unit.

Utility furniture was designed to make best use of available raw materials, as well as being forward-looking in style. Only approved manufacturers could produce it, and the designs were intended to be constructed by a range of makers, small or large, whether by hand or machine. Materials used included plywood, particularly oak, but also recycled materials. Vast quantities of Utility furniture were made, with 25,000 pieces produced in the first two months of the scheme.

Despite being made with sparing use of resources, Utility furniture was intended to last a lifetime, and featured strongly in the 1950s home. The furniture consisted of simple, unornamented designs with minimal upholstery. Textiles featured small patterns (to ensure maximum economy when joining pattern repeats), with the limited colour range of 'rust', green, blue and cream.

Compulsory rationing of furniture had ended in 1948, and design restrictions were lifted after 1952. Consumers had the option to buy new furniture. For those who couldn't afford to, there were plenty of outlets for used furniture – local second-hand shops, advertisements in local newspapers and house contents sales. To make a piece of furniture look more contemporary one could just paint it or change the upholstery.

As spaces inside the modern 1950s home had become much smaller and versatile, the use and design of furniture had to reflect this change. Some pieces of furniture, such as island units (stand-alone storage/worktop units) and room dividers (large sideboards with shelving designed to store items but

Opposite:
A popular stripe-and-pattern wallpaper combination from John Line's 1951 collection, with furniture and decor by Liberty.

Right: The bedroom suite of Utility furniture displayed at the Rural Life Centre, Tilford.

Below left: Colourful kitchen furniture covered with Formica, carefully slotted into a compact kitchen.

Below right: *Practical Householder* advises on how to modernise a Utility bed (showing that Utility furniture was still in wide use at the end of the decade). The economical use of wood in the original Utility design contrasts with the lavish feel of the proposed walnut-veneered version.

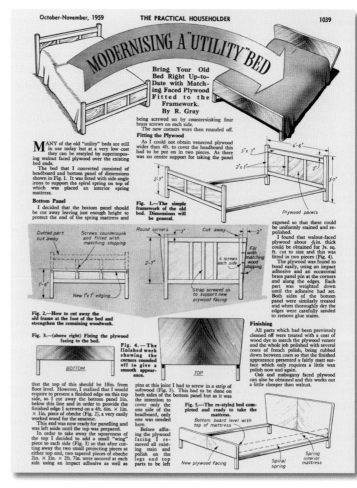

This advertisement for an alternative to the well-known Formica surfacing shows the range of flexible fold-down furniture on which surface plastic could be applied.

Furniture manufacturers extolled the saving of 'space, trouble and time' that fitted furniture would bring.

also dividing up a space) became common where kitchens became kitchen-diners or where sitting rooms became living-dining areas. As the dining room disappeared and families began to eat more often in the kitchen, the dining table moved to the kitchen. People purchased cheap modern fold-away designs, many of which had thermoplastic tops that were lightweight and easy to clean.

Built-in storage was also a popular feature of the 1950s home. Many new homes were already furnished with built-in cupboards and wardrobes – particularly council homes. Built-in furniture was believed

to make best use of space, and of course prevented the need for new inhabitants to buy any.

Modern furniture was flexible and often multi-purpose: sofa beds were popular, as were fold-down table-tops. Magazines suggested making best use of space in the bedroom by using a table hung to the wall that would double up as a writing desk, instead of a traditional dressing table. Light and adjustable styles sold well.

Obtaining modern furniture was not as easy as it might seem, and many people didn't want it. In the early 1950s suppliers were reluctant to experiment with new styles when money was short, preferring to stock pre-war designs and brands guaranteed to sell well. As with décor, at this time of economic uncertainty, and perhaps in reaction to the 'good design' relentlessly imposed by government, many people preferred to return to reproduction furniture in earlier styles. Chunky Tudor-style furniture in dark woods was featured in magazines and elegant Regency antiques were in vogue, as was light-coloured, solid furniture made of beech and elm in the English cottage tradition.

Modes of shopping changed as manufacturers used strong branding to sell their goods. Whereas in previous years department stores had promoted a range of furniture from smaller suppliers of their choice, in the 1950s they began to sell brands of furniture. They therefore lost some of their influence in choosing stock. Nevertheless, independent retailers still carried 50 per cent of the trade in 1954.

A few department stores in London did risk promoting novel designs. Heals and Harrods embraced the new 'contemporary' style for example, although these fashionable stores were beyond the price range of many. The contemporary style was influenced by Scandinavian design – it was wooden, lightweight, clear-cut, colourful and, contrary to traditional furniture, featured splayed legs. 'Scandinavian' style furniture was similar to the contemporary style, but was often made of darker wood and was slightly chunkier. Heals was the first firm to use techniques for veneering wood onto metal – a strong theme in the contemporary look.

Ideas behind modern designs had evolved as early as the 1920s and '30s, but had stalled during the war. With people looking to a bright new future it made sense to introduce new designs, even if these took a while to infiltrate into everyday homes. Many people initially perceived the contemporary style as too modern, cold and uncoordinated for their homes, opting for a traditional three-piece suite. A 1946 Board of Trade survey on furniture revealed that 51 per cent of people preferred suites of furniture, considering them cosier and

These chairs are typically modern in their use of glass-fibre, metal, and coloured leather.

For the more daring of those opting for three-piece suites, two-colour versions were popular.

This advertisement from a 1953 copy of the *Daily Mirror* shows costs and hire purchase costs of furniture in traditional styles.

more comfortable. They also thought suites were more convenient, doubting their ability to combine contemporary pieces tastefully and considered contemporary furniture more for intellectual, artistic classes, rather than the working classes.

The contemporary style encouraged consumers to buy single pieces of furniture rather than sets or suites – to mix and match styles rather than trying hard to coordinate. This had the advantage of being far easier to finance. As most people still favoured traditional three-piece suites, however, they had to pay out a large initial outlay. Suites were difficult to buy without choosing to pay by hire purchase, which meant paying for goods in instalments, with added interest. Still, many people preferred to do this.

Another option was to choose G-Plan furniture, a range introduced by E. Gomme of High Wycombe in 1953. Designed by Donald

G-plan had a strong advertising campaign. This is an image from a G-Plan advertisement, showing the range from dark walnut sideboards to yellow and white tables. Note the stylish simplicity of the layout, parquet flooring and patterned curtains that contrast with the plain walls.

Gomme, it consisted of limited ranges of contemporary-style furniture units intended for use throughout the house. G-Plan furniture was fashionable but more affordable than the single pieces available in more expensive department stores. Each range remained in production for years to allow people to collect pieces as they could afford to. In theory people could pick one piece or many pieces from the styles on offer to suit their budget, and coordinate all furniture in their home if they wanted to. Initially furniture was made in oak but later in teak to imitate the Scandinavian style. G-Plan was one of Britain's largest furniture manufacturers in the 1950s. The concept of unit furniture became very popular and was soon produced by competing suppliers.

By the end of the 1950s contemporary furniture had become widely adopted. *Homes and Gardens* magazine (September 1958) acknowledged influences from other countries (mainly Scandinavia) but insisted that the British had finally got the hang of the contemporary style:

Furniture manufacturers such as Minty promoted expanding and interlocking bookcases. Homeowners could buy as many units as they needed for their room.

This kitchen-diner is furnished with a very modern range of simple and matching units. The display of glass on the sideboard complements the contemporary style well. Note the vinyl flooring, mix of patterned and plain walls, and fashionable and practical blind.

In Britain our talent is for making warm, welcoming homes. Our climate is cheerless and our houses cold…and to compensate for this we have developed an informal, cosy style of furnishings. We like the warm textures of thick piled carpets, papered walls, and the comfortable welcome of fully upholstered chairs. It is because of this preference that many people at first thought contemporary furniture looked cold. But I think we have now assimilated the new trends and translated them into our particular style…modern furniture and decorations are used which still retain our traditional homeliness.

These fireside chairs, bureau, coffee table and plastic weave chair were all bought to set up home in the 1950s. The curved plywood arms were very stylish, as were the delicately angled legs.

As contemporary-style furniture became progressively affordable and accepted, more people began to furnish their homes in this way. Manufacturing techniques meant that by the end of the 1950s, people had a greater choice of cheaper furniture in a range of styles, so could pick and choose to suit their tastes and the style of their home.

DECOR

THE 1950s home was a mixture of old and new. Ideas and technology introduced before the Second World War had slowly begun to be incorporated into people's homes. People in older houses often made their homes look more contemporary in cheap and easy ways, by applying bright new paint colours, for example.

DIY consumed the nation in the 1950s. More people owned their own houses than ever before, which gave them a new impetus to decorate. By 1950 almost half of all houses in Britain were at least sixty-five years old and therefore in need of renovation. Labour had become more expensive and builders less available. People had new materials, technology, time and money at their fingertips. All of these factors persuaded more homeowners to decorate their homes themselves. Both men and women got involved. New magazines such as *Practical Householder*, first published in 1955, encouraged this vogue for DIY. It also featured on television, with handyman W. P. Matthew starring regularly from as early as 1939, to be replaced from 1956 by the popular show, 'Barry Bucknell's Do It Yourself', watched by 7 million viewers.

The rise in popularity of DIY altered the way that people valued their homes and allowed them to make changes on minimal budgets. This began in the post-war era, spurred on by magazines in the 'Make-do and Mend' mindset – to redecorate without professional help, to instil new life into a home simply and cheaply, and to make furniture for the home out of odds and ends. By the end of the decade, however, magazines had embraced consumerism, insisting that new colours, décor and appliances were desirable. To accompany the take-up of DIY, new shops aimed at the DIY market sprang up alongside traditional building merchants. Tool manufacturers including Black and Decker and Wolf began to produce tools for the home market, such as power drills and workbenches.

New emulsion paints replaced distemper (an oil-bound paint first produced commercially in the early nineteenth century), enabling colour to be applied faster and less messily, in only one coat. New brushes and rollers designed for the DIY enthusiast made painting easier.

Opposite:
Curtain fabric,
c. 1955, in typical
1950s colours of
grey and yellow.

Right: Interior view of a new build in Brimsdown, Enfield, 1958, showing a bold tiled fireplace, contemporary wallpaper and sparse ornamentation.

Below right: Magazines such as *Practical Householder* encouraged their readership to build and renovate houses, but also to make and mend furniture.

Below far right: Vinyl and thermoplastic floor tiles came in many colours and designs. In this advertisement women are being targeted to undertake DIY.

Below: Power tool manufacturers such as Black and Decker nurtured their new market of homeowners.

Many people recall the drab colours that dominated the housing landscape in the 1950s. Wartime shortages and large quantities of council housing with prescribed limited colour schemes meant that browns, beiges and greys were common. Houses that had suffered bomb damage were eligible for county grants for refurbishment. Homeowners then had a small choice of wallpapers, mostly beige.

To counter this, bright and contrasting colours became increasingly popular inside people's homes throughout the decade, easily applied by homeowners themselves. Noel Carrington in *Colour and Pattern in the Home* (1954) remarks:

> Our interiors of today often depend rather more on colour than on architectural form. This is perhaps not the fault of the architect. He has to build for economy, both in terms of space and money.... He therefore resorts to colour to improve or add variety to an interior.

Magazines began to issue their own brands of paint colours. *House and Garden* (March 1956) promotes its new range as 'infinitely flexible … a very noticeable trend towards softer, gentler backgrounds, with vivid, bright colours as accents…. Strong and gentle are not mutually exclusive; both can give you intense pleasure if you use them aright.'

The plans of an architect-built house in Rugby in 1957 specify a diverse paint scheme: a kitchen with cloud grey walls and sunshine yellow doors; a three-colour lounge with white woodwork and opal green walls, aside from one wall which is 'sea spray' to match the ceiling. The landing and hall are grey and pink. Outside, the garage and house doors are pale primrose. The *News of theWorld Better Homes Book* (*c.* 1954) suggested a range of colourful decorating schemes, including for the bathroom, 'jade green bath and other fittings; walls, ceiling and paintwork white; floor, dark green rubber or linoleum; curtains and bath-mat, tomato red or lemon yellow.'

Alongside paint, wallpaper was also revolutionised in the 1950s. Previously, it was sold with selvedges that had to be trimmed. In the 1950s, however, ready- or semi-trimmed papers were sold, along with the introduction in 1953 of easy mix water-soluble, cellulose-based wallpaper paste. Paper was still rationed in the early 1950s, but the Council of Industrial Design and later the popular press encouraged the use of modern patterned papers combined with contrasting patterns or painted sections of wall. It was fashionable to have three walls painted or wallpapered with one plain colour, and the fourth wall wallpapered with a patterned design. The nineteenth-century company Wallpaper Manufacturers Ltd (or WPM) still accounted for 60–70 per cent of all wallpaper sales in 1950s Britain.

Besides the huge range of wallpapers and paints, other fashionable surfaces for cladding walls included wood panels, which had the added advantage of further insulating the room and, for bathrooms in particular, tiles in bright colours.

Décor in the kitchen became brighter, with an emphasis on cleanliness and easy maintenance. In his book *Design and Decoration*

Paint swatches showing the *House & Garden* colours of 1957.

This wallpaper company promotes the use of daring colour and pattern in the bathroom.

'Montacute' wallpaper designed by Robert Nicholson for WPM, 1958.

in the Home (1952), Noel Carrington advised a 'less austere and more decorative background … such as can be given by an open dresser with decorative pottery or a gay tablecloth.' Modernising kitchens could be done quite easily using newly available DIY materials. Rather than splash out on a brand new fitted kitchen, new and old units could be repainted in one colour. Wipe-clean wallpaper was available and PVC was used to make new curtains. Formica was the modern and colourful plastic heat-resistant covering that could be applied to surfaces such as worktops and tables to give them a new lease of life. It was made from thermal-set paper or fabric impregnated with melamine resin, could be applied with glue, and had a wipe-clean, scratch-resistant and durable surface.

Tiles were also used on fireplaces to modernise a decorative scheme in the 1950s. This article explains how to update an older style.

Formica – a plastic covering – was promoted as a modern and convenient surface to brighten up a range of spaces in the home.

'Wicklow', floral chintz fabric sample, Fothergay Ltd, c. 1955.

As was the case with modern furniture, many consumers did reject contemporary trends in decorating in favour of reproductions of earlier fabrics and wallpapers. Revival styles were very popular. In a booklet from the early 1950s entitled *Furnishing the Living Room*, the Times Furnishing Company advocates a period style room in order to 'escape from the rush and turmoil of today'.

The cottage style was common, with white walls and revealed wooden beams, soft pastel colours such as yellows, cream and blues, and printed floral or sampler designs on chintz and wallpapers. Cottage-style wallpaper

Interior of a dining room at the 1959 Daily Mail Ideal Home Show, incorporating a fitted carpet. Ceramics are displayed.

A rag rug warms up the lino floor in this teenager's bedroom, as displayed in the Sandling Farmhouse at the Museum of Kent Life.

was a bestseller in the 1950s. Late eighteenth- and early nineteenth-century styles came back into fashion too for those that could afford them. Wallpaper was key to these schemes. Expensive pin-striped wallpaper and elegant dark wood furniture characterised the formal Regency style, for example.

Fitted carpets came into popular use, easier to clean thanks to the wider ownership of vacuum cleaners, and cheaper due to improved production methods and new synthetic materials. They were still costly, and were used mainly for living rooms that needed to be cosier. Rag rugs, widely used in the 1940s and often handmade, were still prevalent. Arguably the most common

flooring remained linoleum, a natural material introduced in the nineteenth century and made principally of linseed oil. Although it was easy to clean and durable, it was cold underfoot, and it often needed to be covered with rugs. It was frequently used in hallways, landings and kitchens, with tile patterns in colours such as cream and green. Newly produced flooring such as vinyl tiles were also used to provide a colourful, cheaper and practical alternative to carpets. At the upper, designer end of the scale, natural materials such as cork or wood were favoured, used without rugs for an uncluttered look in living rooms.

Printed textiles typify the 1950s. They were blasted into a new realm by contemporary artists such as Lucienne Day and Jacqueline Groag, who created influential designs for big stores like Heals and Selfridges and manufacturers such as David Whitehead Fabrics. Many designs were characterised by bright colours and quirky discursive patterns. The main export markets at the time, Australia and South Africa, influenced this change. At the start of the decade, contrasting colours, figurative lines and abstract patterns were in fashion. By the end of the decade the look was more mottled, although it retained strong pattern and colour.

Key designs were transferred to all sorts of surfaces including upholstery, curtains, carpets, wallpaper and crockery. Towards the end of the 1950s these designs were duly being copied for the mass market. Copies and cheaper modes of manufacture made the contemporary aesthetic available to all.

Different types of textiles were used in each space in the house. *Housewife* magazine (March 1955) advises:

Colourful and practical ceramics were popular in the 1950s. This advertisement dates from 1959, by which time the contemporary aesthetic was available to all.

> In a bedroom, hall or dining room, you can have a less expensive fabric, since there is not so much wear and tear. Money saved in this way can be put to better and harder-wearing fabrics for the living room, which takes the full brunt of family life. Children's rooms should have fabrics that are gay and pretty; nothing heavy or dull. Bathrooms and kitchens are a natural home for plastics, cottons or cotton and rayon mixtures, and, as with children's rooms, easy-to-clean is one of the main requirements.

The press insisted that where a room featured heavily designed wallpaper or tiles around a fireplace, fabrics, upholstery and rugs should be unpatterned. If the walls were plain, then the textiles could be highly decorative.

The newly available cheaper synthetic fabrics must have been a revelation to the consumer. Rayon was used widely for soft furnishings and satins but nylon was still mainly confined to clothing. Bedding was still made of cotton and wool. Cotton sheets were used with woollen or cotton candlewick bedspreads of differing designs.

Many homeowners bought their own fabrics at department stores in order to upholster, make curtains and decorate rooms. Fabric was a

A bedroom at the
1958 Daily Mail
Ideal Home Show.

straightforward way to revamp a space. *Ideal Home* advocated draping fabric over the bedstead to create a feeling of luxury.

The contemporary aesthetic was generally uncluttered. Clean lines were favoured with minimal ornamentation – not only stylish, but a practical concern in smaller homes. In contrast to the Victorian preference for many ornaments, it was fashionable to display a few choice pieces of pottery and glass, and perhaps some large houseplants. Pelmets and picture lights were increasingly discarded, considered impractical to clean and unnecessary.

Bedroom textiles
were luxurious.
This is an example
of the widely used
candlewick
bedspreads.

GARDENS

IN THE newer homes in the early 1950s gardens were usually a low priority, as householders struggled to furnish and decorate their interiors first. New family houses were designed with relatively big gardens because in the modernist tradition, fresh air was viewed as a necessity for children.

As rationing lingered and food was far from abundant, people used their outdoor spaces for growing vegetables and fruit, and for keeping poultry. Gardens were no longer used to 'Dig for Victory' to the same extent as in wartime Britain though. Anderson shelters, bomb shelters issued free by the government to those eligible during the Second World War, frequently remained in gardens, used as sheds or simply abandoned.

Gardens of the 1950s incorporated working areas – as well as a vegetable patch, there was usually a designated place for washing to dry and a space where babies would sleep in their prams or children would play. Pathways separated these different spaces – crazy paving was a fashionable feature.

In many gardens, priority was given to lawns, with bedding plants neatly contained in the borders for spring and summer flowering. Flowers such as climbing roses were very popular, as were trees and shrubs such as rhododendrons and azaleas.

Gardens became an important part of the home environment. In the *Daily Mail Ideal Home Book* of 1951–2, Alex Morley-Smith claims that his new garden 'has always been considered very much part of the home, and has been part of the whole plan as far as finances and "furnishing" are concerned... Where there is such a narrow garden frontage there is no room for a "sordid" bit.'

By the end of the decade, as austerity began to cave in to

A garden in Lincolnshire, 1952. The front garden was given over to lawn and border planting, but there was a large vegetable garden too.

Above: Gardens were a luxury for many. They delighted owners of the new prefab houses.

Above right: The garden of a house in Essex, built in 1956, typical for its lawn, pathways, and rocky walls.

leisure and commercialism, the garden had been widely adopted as a space for the whole family to relax in. Magazines such as *Homes and Gardens* (June 1958) were running articles on 'Living out-of-doors', promoting the latest ranges of garden furniture and infusing the reader with images of happy scenes of alfresco living. They urged the reader to use outdoor spaces:

> Your terrace may be part of a sweeping view.... But even if it is a back yard, a balcony, or the roof of a garage, it is just as precious to its owner on those wonderful days when the sun shines, and you abandon household chores and take every possible meal in the open air....

Sitting out in the garden, enjoying the fresh air. Behind you can see that the garden is mostly lawn, with new shrubs in the borders and a concrete path.

CONCLUSION

Aʟᴛʜᴏᴜɢʜ some of the idealistic homes of the 1950s have not survived, such as the high-rise flats destroyed following safety concerns, most 1950s buildings are still in use, maintaining their open-plan layouts and simple designs that remain convenient today. In the earlier part of the decade especially, the government clearly influenced design and architecture in a new and powerful way, acting, it believed, in the nation's best interests.

New towns and prefabs, largely planned in the 1940s, were a huge feature of 1950s Britain, and the majority of people were overjoyed with their new homes, despite having to move long distances in many cases. Housing was greatly improved, with many of the working and middle classes moving into homes equipped with the latest technology.

Collectively, people witnessed a sea change in the way that they lived. The convenience and ease of our lifestyles today began for the wider population in the 1950s – with plumbing, new technology and materials, consumer choice, and easier routes to home ownership. We now realise the need to curb the consumerism that has taken over since the 1950s, and appreciate the economically designed homes from that decade, made to be proud of, and made to last.

A house designed by Davis contractors at the 1958 Ideal Home show.

FURTHER READING

Balchin, Paul, and Rhoden, Maureen (editors). *Housing: The Essential Foundations*. Routledge, 1998.

Bingham, Neil, and Weaving, Andrew. *Modern Retro: Living with Mid-Century Modern Style*. Ryland Peters & Small Ltd, 2005.

Colquhoun, Ian. *RIBA Book of British Housing: 1900 to the Present Day*. Architectural Press, 2008.

Fiell, Charlotte, and Fiell, Peter. *Modern Furniture Classics: Postwar to Post-modernism*. Thames and Hudson, 2001.

Hoskins, Lesley. *Fiftiestyle: Home Decoration and Furnishing from the 1950s*. MODA, Middlesex University Press, 2004. (A very useful overview.)

Hyman, Basil, and Braggs, Steven. *The G-Plan Revolution: A Celebration of British Popular Furniture of the 1950s and 1960s*. Booth-Clibborn Editions, 2007.

Jackson, Lesley. *The New Look: Design in the Fifties*. Thames and Hudson, 1991.

Jackson, Lesley. *Contemporary Architecture and Interiors of the 1950s*. Phaidon Press Ltd, 1998.

London County Council. *A survey of post-war housing of the LCC 1945–1959*. LCC, 1959.

MacDonald, Sally, and Porter, Julia. *Putting on the Style: Setting up Home in the 1950s*. The Geffrye Museum, London, 1990. (An extremely comprehensive look at the 1950s home, focusing on London.)

Power, Anne. *Hovels to High Rise: State Housing in Europe since 1850*. Routledge, 1993.

Quinn, Bradley. *Mid-Century Modern*. Conran Octopus Ltd, 2004.

Ryan, Deborah S. *The Ideal Home Through the 20th Century: Daily Mail Ideal Home Exhibition*. Hazar Publishing, 1997.

English Heritage has a range of relevant publications, including their information leaflet, *Something Worth Keeping – Post-war architecture in England*, which is available online at the time of printing, at: www.english-heritage.org.uk/server/show/nav.19027

PLACES TO VISIT

Design Museum, Shad Thames, London SE1 2YD.
 Telephone: 0870 833 9955. Website: www.designmuseum.org
Geffrye Museum, Kingsland Road, London E2 8EA.
 Telephone: +44 (0)20 7739 9893. Website: www.geffrye-museum.org.uk
Kettle's Yard, Castle Street, Cambridge CB3 0AQ. Telephone: +44 (0)1223
 748100. Website: www.kettlesyard.co.uk
MoDA (The Museum of Domestic Design & Architecture), Middlesex University,
 Cat Hill, Barnet, Hertfordshire EN4 8HT. Telephone: +44 (0)20 8411
 5244. Website: www.moda.mdx.ac.uk
Museum of the 50s Era, Cae Dai Trust, Denbigh, Denbighshire,
 Wales LL16 4SU. Telephone: 01745 817004. Website:
 www.hiraethog.org.uk
Victoria and Albert Museum, Cromwell Road, London SW7 2RL.
 Telephone: +44 (0)20 7942 2000. Website: www.vam.ac.uk

NATIONAL TRUST PROPERTIES:
20 Forthlin Road, Allerton, Liverpool L24 1YP. Telephone: 0844 800
 4791. Website: www.nationaltrust.org.uk (as with all NT properties).
Birmingham Back to Backs, 50–54 Inge Street/55–63 Hurst Street,
 Birmingham, West Midlands B5 4TE. Telephone: 0121 666 7671.
Mendips, Woolton, Liverpool L25 7SA. Telephone: 0844 800 4791.
Mr Hardman's Photographic Studio, 59 Rodney Street, Liverpool L1 9EX.
 Telephone: 0151 709 6261.

Readers may also like to contact:
The Design History Society.
 Website: www.designhistorysociety.org
 Email: membership@designhistory.org
The Twentieth Century Society, 70 Cowcross Street, London EC1M 6EJ.
 Telephone: 020 7250 3857. Website: www.c20society.org.uk

INDEX

Page numbers in italics refer to illustrations